Out of Season

Kari Jones

Orca currents

ORCA BOOK PUBLISHERS

Library and Archives Canada Cataloguing in Publication

Jones, Kari, 1966-
Out of season / Kari Jones.

(Orca currents)
Issued also in electronic formats.
ISBN 978-1-4598-0097-7 (bound).--ISBN 978-1-4598-0096-0 (pbk.)

I. Title. II. Series: Orca currents
PS8619.O5328O98 2012   jC813'.6   C2011-907788-4

First published in the United States, 2012
Library of Congress Control Number: 2011943723

Summary: Fourteen-year-old Maya uses her kayaking skills
to save a family of sea otters from poachers.

*Orca Book Publishers is dedicated to preserving the environment and has
printed this book on paper certified by the Forest Stewardship Council®.*

Orca Book Publishers gratefully acknowledges the support for its
publishing programs provided by the following agencies: the Government
of Canada through the Canada Book Fund and the Canada Council for the Arts,
and the Province of British Columbia through the BC Arts Council
and the Book Publishing Tax Credit.

Cover photography by Getty Images
Author photo by Ryan Rock

ORCA BOOK PUBLISHERS
PO Box 5626, Stn. B
Victoria, BC Canada
V8R 6S4

ORCA BOOK PUBLISHERS
PO Box 468
Custer, WA USA
98240-0468

www.orcabook.com
Printed and bound in Canada.

15 14 13 12 • 4 3 2 1

To Wyatt, in welcome

Chapter One

I hear Dad's motor roar off across the bay, and I know it's time. I close the back door with a click and wait to make sure I didn't wake Mom, then tiptoe across the yard to the dock. My life jacket fits easily over my head. I slide the kayak into the water. In the early morning gray, the boat looks like a seal slipping off a rock.

I dip my paddle into the water and glide away from shore, keeping to the shoreline to hide under overhanging tree branches and behind rocks. When I'm far enough away from the house that I can make some noise, I dig my paddle into the water harder. The kayak surges forward. On a calm day like today, I can be out of Oyster Bay and around Rugged Point in ten minutes. Then it's only another ten minutes to Riley Bay, where the sea otters live in the kelp beds. I can spend an hour with them before Mom notices I'm missing.

Mom would have a fit if she knew I was doing this. She'd worry I'd get hurt. She'd imagine rogue waves carrying me out to sea or angry sea lions biting my boat in half. She's like that, my mom. Dad's not. He taught me to kayak. I'll tell him about these trips soon, but for now, this time with the sea otters is all mine.

I round the headland, leaning into the sudden wind. I curve the boat tightly around the rocks and into Riley Bay. As soon as I'm in the bay, I relax and paddle more slowly.

I've been coming out here for five days now, and every morning I wonder if the sea otters are still going to be here. So far, I haven't heard anyone at school or in town mention them. I hope I'm the only one who knows about them. If someone finds out, the sea otters could die.

Last year a fisherman shot a sea otter farther up the coast. He said it was destroying the catch. That's what happens to animals that eat fish around here. No one has time for them.

Having sea otters is a gift. They're so beautiful, and rare.

There is no way I'm letting anything happen to them, even if I have to check on them every day for the rest of my life.

Riley Bay is full of rocks and tiny islands and a long kelp bed. The sloping hills block the sun, so I don't see the sea otters until I'm almost on top of them. Their black heads look like bull kelp bulbs. Their flippers are like waving seaweed. Most people wouldn't notice them at all. They are the most beautiful animals I've ever seen. They have black eyes and teddy-bear snouts, and they curve and twist in the water like acrobats when they play in the waves. They're smart too. They use rocks to crush sea urchins.

Today they're resting in the kelp.

"Hey, guys," I say. They know I'm here. I'm sure of it. They're relaxing, so I relax too. I balance my paddle across my cockpit and lean forward.

Two of the otters swim toward me. They lie on their backs, looking up. One is bigger than the other, almost as big as me. They've wrapped their flippers together like they're holding hands.

"Hi, Gertrude. Hi, Oscar," I say. They look at me but don't swim any closer. "How's the fishing?" I want to reach out and stroke their cute noses, but I know better than that, so I splash the water next to the kayak instead. Lilly, the smaller otter, slaps the water with her tail.

I could stay here forever watching these guys play, but it's not long before a shot of sunlight sprays over the hills of Riley Bay, and I know I should head home.

But Gertrude is eating another sea urchin. I have to watch her smack open the shell against a rock on her tummy, then scrape out the flesh by holding it to her mouth with her flippers. She uses her teeth as fingers to grab the meat inside. When she's done, I look up to see the sun is too high in the sky.

If I don't hurry, I'll be late.

I put my paddle in the water and take a stroke. The otters back away and watch me. I take one last look, then turn the kayak toward home. As the kayak glides forward, I glance up to the hillside, and my stroke falters. Someone is standing at the top of the hill. I can't tell who it is, but they're watching me play with the sea otters.

Chapter Two

What have I done? With two strokes I move behind the shelter of a rock. My heart races. Who was that? What did they see? I pray that it's not the same fisherman who shot the sea otters last year.

I can't leave now. I sneak between two rocks in the middle of Riley Bay so I can get a better view of the person on the hill. I've never seen anyone up there before.

Why would someone be at the top of the hill early in the morning? We're far from town, and no one lives around here. There are no roads. The only access is by boat. There is nothing out here except trees and rocks—and sea otters.

My stomach clenches. Have I given the sea otters away? Are they in danger now?

What should I do?

I'm going to be late. If I'm late, I might be grounded, and I won't be able to watch out for the sea otters. I look up again. The person walks along the ridge to the crest of the hill, then disappears into the trees.

"Arghh…" I shout into the bay. I turn my kayak and race home.

When I get close to the house, I see Dad's boat at the dock. Mom must have called Dad and Saul home. That means she noticed I was missing. There isn't any point in pretending. I pull my kayak up onto the dock, take off my life jacket and walk in the back door.

I'm not happy when I see everyone sitting around the table. There's no doubt about it, I'm in trouble. Dad and Saul only come in for breakfast if there are no fish, or if something bad has happened. I guess I'm the something bad today.

Saul smirks when he sees me. He's four years older than me, and now that he's out of school, he's Dad's fishing partner. He thinks that makes him better than me. Dad lifts his eyebrows. Mom says, "Where have you been? I thought you were still in bed."

Before I can answer, Saul says, "Kayaking."

Thanks, Saul. Sometimes having an older brother is frustrating. I was going to say, "Out walking." Too late now.

"Kayaking? Alone? Maya, how could you? You know how I feel about you being out there alone. Anything could happen. Gerry, did you know about this?" Mom turns to Dad. So do I.

Dad will understand. He taught me how to kayak so I could explore. He gets why I kayak in the mornings. I want to say, "Tell her it's okay, Dad."

Before I can open my mouth, Dad lifts his fork and waves it at me. "You stay away from that kayak, Maya."

"But…"

"No buts. Your mother doesn't want you out there. You stay off the water or there will be consequences." He lowers his fork and spears some egg.

Tears hit the back of my eyes. "Dad?" I say.

He doesn't look at me as he eats his eggs. I glance at Saul, but he's nodding like he agrees with Dad.

"Stay away from the kayak, Maya," Dad says, glancing up from his food. There's something funny about his face. This is so unlike him. It's so unfair. My face burns, and I have a lump in my throat from trying not to cry.

"What were you doing out there anyway?" asks Saul.

I don't want to answer, but Mom and Dad are watching me. I would have told them about the sea otters. I would have. But now I'm not going to. "Looking around. There are seals on Princess Rock," I say.

It's not a lie, but it's not the truth.

My voice cracks as I say, "I need to get ready for school."

For the rest of the morning I have to think of other things, or I want to cry. Why did Dad turn on me? I know Mom worries. I'm okay with that. But I thought Dad was on my side. Why did he betray me?

Chapter Three

I lie awake. Why did Dad tell me to stay away from the kayak? He's being such a jerk. It's not fair. He'd never say something like that to Saul.

He taught me to kayak. He knows how much I love watching animals. With each thought, my breath grows sharper. I want to fling my pillow across the room. What will happen to the sea otters if no one watches out for them?

Nothing. I won't let it.

By morning I'm worn out, but I've made a decision. I can't abandon the sea otters now that someone knows about them. I can't stop now, no matter what Dad says. Dad's wrong. That's all there is to it. I'm going to have to be more careful, that's all.

I wait until Dad and Saul are gone, then creep out of the house. My heart beats so fast I have to put my hand over my chest to still it. No lights turn on when I close the door. I take a deep breath and check my heart again. Without looking back, I sprint across the lawn. At the dock I slip into my life jacket and slide the kayak into the water. It hardly makes a splash. I edge into the cockpit and push off. I'm going to paddle to the sea otters and make sure they're okay and then kayak back. That's all I'm going to do. No one will miss me.

I see the sea otters as soon as I round the headland into Riley Bay. "Hey, guys," I call. I smile, and my shoulders relax. Until I look up.

Someone is standing at the top of the hill.

Again!

My hands shake as I grasp the paddle harder and steer my kayak away from the kelp bed. Maybe if I paddle across the bay without stopping, the man on the hillside won't see the sea otters.

Or maybe he already has.

I have to find out. It's the only way to make sure the sea otters are safe.

It only takes me a second to paddle to shore and pull my kayak onto the rocks. What am I doing? I must be crazy.

I have no idea what this man is doing up there. I turn around. But then I think of the sea otters.

What if he catches them?

Or worse, shoots them?

It makes me sick to think about it. There's nothing else to do. I start up the hill before I can change my mind.

The hill is steep, but there are lots of tree trunks to hold on to. As I climb, I think about what I will do when I reach the top. I'll just talk to the man, ask him what he's doing. We'll be two innocent people meeting on a hilltop.

Right. If only I can convince my breathing of that.

I'm about to rise over the crest of the hill when my foot slips, and I step on a twig. It cracks. I jump. My head hits a branch. I stuff my hand into my mouth before I cry out.

When my head stops hurting and my heart slows, I stand up and peer over the hilltop. The man is running along the crest of the hill. He turns into the woods. Without thinking, I scramble up the last steps to the top of the hill and follow him. There are huge footprints in the mud near the edge of the trees. I track them for ten paces into the woods. Then they disappear. I spin around. Where has he gone?

He's vanished.

The forest is dense. I can't see a path. I pace across the top of the hill. How could I let him get away?

I want to shout in frustration, but there is no point. Whoever it was is gone. If I don't leave soon, I'll be late.

That would not be good.

I don't want to learn what consequences Dad has planned for me. I take one last look around, then head back down the hill.

It's harder going down than it had been coming up. Each step is more like a slide. I have to grab tree trunks to stop myself from slipping down the hill and into the water. By the time I reach the bottom, my shoes are covered in dirt and my hands are sticky with tree sap. I rinse them in the ocean so Mom and Dad won't notice.

I pull my kayak into the water and paddle around the rocks for a last look at the sea otters. Today they're ignoring me. They don't move when I paddle close.

"Hi, guys" I say. "I can't stay today, but I'll come back tomorrow. I promise. I'm going to find out what's going on. You be careful, okay?" I count one, two, three sea otters before I leave.

I race home, letting my anger guide my paddle.

"How." Stroke.

"Could." Stroke.

"I." Stroke.

"Let." Stroke.

"This." Stroke.

"Happen?" Stroke.

Each stroke works away a bit of frustration.

By the time I turn into Oyster Bay, I'm short of breath and my arms ache. I slow down.

I hope Mom isn't up yet, but in case she is, I hug the shoreline. The overhanging tree branches hide my kayak. When I'm almost home, Dad's boat roars into the bay. He shoots across the water to our dock.

He's driving too fast.

When he throttles down, he shoots a spray behind him. He almost hits the dock.

It's not like Dad to drive like that. What is going on? For a second I think he knows I was out kayaking. A huge sob fills my mouth.

What will he do?

I bite back the sob.

I stay under the branches while Dad and Saul get out of the boat. Neither of them speaks as they walk along the dock. They give me no clues.

When Dad and Saul are in the house, I come out from behind the tree branches. I don't pull my kayak onto the dock in case they notice it when they come back. Instead, I hide it behind the boat shed.

I run around the house and to the porch. I smooth down my hair and straighten my clothes, then lower myself into Mom's chair and wait for someone to call me to breakfast.

It feels rotten to be sneaky.

It doesn't take long before Mom's voice calls out, "Maya, breakfast." I'm about to open the door when I remember my wet shoes. I take them off and throw them onto the mat, hoping no one will notice them until they've dried. I take a deep breath and head inside.

Saul is in the hallway. "Stop," he says as I try to squeeze past.

"What?" I ask.

He looks at his feet and shrugs, "Mom's worried about you. You should stop."

"Stop what?" I say, looking right at his face.

"You know what."

"No, I don't. Tell me. What should I stop?"

"You know. Kayaking."

How did he know? My clothing is dry. I took off my wet shoes. I smoothed down my hair. "What makes you think I've been kayaking?" I ask.

Saul huffs. "Just stop it, okay?"

"What I do is none of your business, Saul," I say, and I try to squeeze past again.

Saul grabs my arm and pushes me against the wall. "Stop kayaking, Maya, or I'll tell Dad."

I yank my arm away from him and shove past. "Mind your own business, Saul," I say. My voice sounds strong, but inside, my whole body is shaking.

The whole morning has been freaky. Who was the person on the hillside? Why did he run away? And most of all, why is Saul acting so strange?

Chapter Four

I have to figure out what's going on. There are so many questions chasing each other in my mind that I can't concentrate at school. In science I almost walk into the skeleton hanging by the window, and in socials I drop a pile of books on my toes. In English I can't remember what *onomatopoeia* means.

I'm too busy thinking about what to do about the sea otters. Usually, I'd talk to Dad about this.

Obviously that's not going to work.

I'm concerned about him too.

At lunchtime I spill apple juice all over myself. I give up trying to act normal and sit in a corner to make a plan.

At dinner I say, "Mom, I have some extra work to do at school tomorrow. I'm going in early, so don't expect me for breakfast."

Everyone at the table stares at me. They're not convinced. I put on an extra-innocent face.

Mom says, "Okay, honey. It's about time you started concentrating on school again."

My face burns. I have to look at my plate so no one will notice. Saul kicks me under the table, but I move my leg and pretend I didn't notice. After dinner, I go to my bedroom to get ready. I throw binoculars and my cell phone into my backpack. Before I fall asleep, I set my alarm for 4:30 AM.

When the alarm rings, I almost turn it off and go back to sleep.

Then I remember my plan.

I lie still to make sure no one else in the house is moving.

The house is silent.

Without turning on the light, I dress and grab my backpack. I have to feel my way along the hall and down the stairs. At the door I fumble for my shoes. I open the door an inch at a time. I don't want to make any noise.

My kayak is still behind the shed. I pull it to the water and slide it in. It makes a small splash when I let go of the stern.

I freeze. Nothing moves. My hands shake as I climb into the kayak, but nothing is going to stop me now. In ten strokes I'm under the trees and on my way.

Dawn is just breaking. There's barely enough light to distinguish sea from land. My heart thumps. I force my hands to keep calm on the paddle. The kayak glides through the water, slick as a seal. I'm quiet but not fast.

I glance behind me. In the dark, there's nothing to see. I lean forward and put on the speed. My stomach muscles tense, and I breathe deeply to give myself more power. I have to get there before anyone else does.

When I reach Riley Bay, I head straight for the kelp beds to check on the otters.

"Hi, guys," I whisper, even though no one is around. "I'm on a mission today, so I can't stay and play." I splash water in their direction. They ignore me and keep eating sea urchins. "Silly," I say, but I'm glad they're okay.

There's enough light now to see the shore. I climb out of the kayak and drag it past the rocks, then arrange branches over it. You'd have to look closely to see it was there. I brush my tracks in the mud with a pine branch to mask them. As fast as I can, I hike to the hilltop and hide behind a tree.

Now that I'm still, I think about what might happen if Dad finds out I'm here. He'll be furious, that's for sure. It's tempting to head home and go back to bed and forget about all of this. But then I remember the sea otters. They need me to keep them safe. Until I find out what the man on the hill is doing, I'm not going anywhere. I sit up straighter and wait.

The sun is still hiding behind the hill when Dad's boat motors into the bay.

What's he doing here? Does he know I'm here? Oh no! Dad stops the motor, and Saul hops onto shore. Dad waves and takes the boat out into the bay.

I sink back into the tree trunk. Honestly, this was the last thing in the world I expected.

What are they doing?

Are they spying on me?

Chapter Five

Dad and Saul! How can it be? I'm so shocked, I can hardly make my arms and legs move. Spying on me. How could they?

Anger rises up my face like a red tide. I clench my hands. I'll show them what it feels like to be spied on.

When Saul reaches the top of the hill, he's disguised in the oversized hoodie he was wearing yesterday. Did he think he could hide from me in that?

Saul sits on a stump. He stares out to sea.

Waiting for me, I bet.

I stand up and push off the tree. I'm going to demand an explanation.

Then I get a better idea. I'll watch him for a while. Then when I do confront him, he'll know what it's like to be watched.

I creep closer to Saul, staying behind trees so he can't see me. Saul doesn't move. I can see the sea otters clearly. He doesn't seem to have noticed them. Maybe I can only see them because I know they're there. Maybe he's not here about the sea otters at all.

Maybe he's only here to spy on me.

Something in my stomach hurts when I think that.

Saul doesn't move at all. Is he waiting for me? How many days has he been doing this? How did he and Dad know I was coming here? That hurt in my stomach grows and grows.

Then Saul stands up and shouts into his radio, "Dad, they're here."

What?

My head whips around. What's he looking at?

A motorboat roars into the channel across from Riley Bay and Rugged Point. What does this mean? Whose boat is that?

You mean he's not looking for me? The question pushes at the space in my stomach where the hurt is. I turn the VHF radio on my life jacket on low.

It's hard to see. I pull my binoculars out of my backpack and focus. The boat moves across the water until it's in the middle of the channel, then stops. There are two men on board. I put the binoculars down.

What is going on? Why would Saul want to tell Dad about this boat?

Then Dad's boat, *Storm Tide*, comes into view. He pulls up beside the other boat. I put the binoculars back up to my eyes to watch.

Dad walks to the back of his boat. He leans forward and points at something on the other boat. The other man waves at him. It's weird, why is he waving at Dad when Dad's right there? Dad says something, and the man shakes both his arms.

Something is wrong.

"Careful, Dad," I whisper.

The man steps toward Dad and pushes him in the chest. Dad staggers back. The man jumps onto his boat. Both Saul and I take a sharp breath. You never ever step onto someone else's boat without an invitation. That doesn't stop the man. He lunges at Dad. Dad shoves him away.

He comes back, arms swinging, and hits Dad in the jaw.

Dad spins. He looks like he's going to fall. He regains his balance and swings at the man.

He misses.

The man bends down and shoves his head into Dad's stomach. He pushes Dad backward until Dad trips over the gunwale of his boat.

Dad falls headfirst into the water.

His boat roars off. The other boat follows.

Dad is alone in the water.

"Dad!" I shout. I can't help it. The word slips out. My mind whirls in confusion. The binoculars in my hands shake.

Saul spins around. "Maya, what…?" He leaps up from the stump. "Go away, Maya. You shouldn't be here."

I know I shouldn't. But Dad's in trouble. I charge down the hill.

"Maya," Saul yells behind me. The two of us speed down the hill.

"What are you doing?" I know Saul's confused. He wants to know what I'm doing here. But I have only one thought on my mind. The water is cold. A swimmer only has five or ten minutes before hypothermia sets in. Dad's a long way out in the channel.

What if he's hurt?

We reach the bottom together. When we slide to a stop, we both have radios to our mouths. Saul says, "Mayday, Mayday, Mayday, this is *Storm Tide* calling. We've got a man overboard. We need help." He's babbling and not following proper Mayday protocol at all.

I can hardly move. "Please, please, please answer," I whisper.

The reply comes. "Is that you, Saul? What's happened?"

"Dad's in the water off Rugged Point. He may be hurt," Saul shouts.

At the word *hurt*, he turns white. We both know it might be worse than that.

"Okay, Saul, Coast Guard Vessel *Marie Celeste* is approximately ten miles south and proceeding to your location. ETA approximately thirty minutes. There are no other vessels nearby. Over."

"Thirty minutes," says Saul.

It's too long.

I know what I have to do.

Chapter Six

I rush to my kayak. I sweep the branches off it, shove it into the water and grab my paddle.

"Maya, no!" calls Saul. He knows what I'm going to do. He lunges to stop me. He misses, and I hop into the kayak.

Saul grabs my stern and pulls the boat back to shore. "Let me go, Maya. I'm stronger. I'll get there faster."

"You won't fit," I say. I look him in the eye. "Saul, let go of my boat. You know you won't fit."

Dad built this boat just for me. Saul is fifty pounds and six inches bigger than I am. He'd tip over the minute he took a forward stroke. Frustration flickers in his eyes. Finally, he lets go. "I can't believe I'm doing this," he says.

I settle into my boat and paddle. Fast.

From the water, I can't see where Dad is. There are rocks and small islands between us. There's no splashing, no flash of moving arms, nothing. Tears blur my vision. I wipe my eyes with my sleeve. The only thing I have to go by is what I saw from the hilltop, so I point my boat in that direction and hope.

Each stroke takes me faster than the one before. Soon I'm flying across the water.

I hope I'm fast enough.

Dad's a good swimmer, but he doesn't have a survival suit on.

What if he's hurt? I can't think about that.

At the mouth of the bay, the current changes. Instead of pushing me toward Dad, it pulls me away from him. I shift my butt back on my seat and lean forward. I push with every muscle, but the boat feels like it's slipping backward. Push, push, push. Each stroke makes my stomach clench and my arms sting. My mouth is dry. All I can think about is getting to Dad.

The boat inches forward. I feel like I'm not moving at all. Sweat pours down my face.

With all of my strength, I pull that paddle again. Suddenly I'm free of the current and in the main channel. Once again the current is working with me.

The boat surges forward.

There's so much water in the channel and no way to tell where to go. It's choppy out here. I don't know where the current has taken Dad. My head spins around, left, right, left, right. I can't see anything to help me locate him. My mind whizzes in a million directions—what if he's drowned? What if I never find him? My stroke falters. Tears blur my vision.

Then my radio crackles. Saul's voice says, "Head west, Maya. I can see him. I'm at the top of the hill. You've got to go to your left."

I've never been so happy to hear Saul's voice in my life.

I angle the bow of my boat left and pull my paddle through the water with all my strength. The kayak turns toward the far shore. After a few strokes, I still can't see anything.

"Farther left, Maya."

I angle the boat more. I still can't see anything. "Saul," I call into my radio. How many minutes has it been?

"You're almost there, Maya," says Saul.

Then I hear Dad. "Maya, over here."

"Where are you?" I scream.

There's no answer. I can't see anything. My mouth turns dry. Did I imagine him calling me? I take another stroke and look around. The chop hits the side of my kayak, threatening to change my angle. I have to look straight ahead again and pay attention.

"Veer right," comes Saul's voice. "You've almost got him."

I change the angle of my boat again and yell, "Dad, are you okay?" My voice is hoarse.

I paddle on, scanning the sea for his head.

"Here," he says. Then I see him. His head is above water.

He hasn't drowned.

All my energy rushes out of me, and I shout in relief, "Saul, I see him!"

The current pushes me west, away from Dad. I gather my energy and shift the angle of the boat. Dip the paddle. Pull. Dip. Pull. He raises his arm so I can keep track of where he is.

In ten strokes I'm alongside him. "Dad, I thought you'd drowned." I am crying, and I can't see anything but my own tears.

"Maya. Thank goodness you ignored me. I have never been so happy to see someone as I am to see you."

I laugh through my tears. "Can you climb onto my stern?"

Dad grabs hold of my boat. With a mighty "hhhffff," he hauls himself up so that his chest lies across the stern. His legs dangle in the water.

The kayak is tippy with Dad's weight on it. I brace with each stroke to keep us upright. The current pushes against me now. My arms burn with the force of paddling. Inch by inch we move closer to shore.

At the change of the current, the waves grow bigger. I brace against them. The current pulls us faster.

"Hold on, Dad," I call.

"I'm holding," he says.

The waves keep coming. A big one hits us broadside, and I throw the paddle into a brace. The wave rolls under us. I straighten the boat and keep paddling. Another wave hits, and another.

My breath comes sharply now. My stomach muscles are clenched. I try to speak to Dad, but I don't have any breath.

"It's rough…" is all that comes out.

"You're doing great, Maya," he yells.

A bigger wave comes at me.

We're not going to make it.

The wave smacks against the boat and breaks over my shoulder. It pushes me along with it. I feel Dad's weight slip off. The boat tips. I go under.

Chapter Seven

I gulp air before my head submerges. With my left hand I swing the paddle alongside the kayak, and then I grab it with my right hand. I flick my hips and push on the paddle. The boat slides under me and rolls upright. My head pops out of the water.

I take a deep breath.

"Dad!" I shout.

"I'm right here. Good job, Maya. That was a great roll."

I can only nod in response.

Dad climbs back onto the stern of my boat, and I paddle again.

When we reach the shore, I'm so cold and exhausted I can't pull the kayak out of the water. Saul wades out as we approach. He helps Dad slide off the stern. Together they stagger to shore. Saul has lit a fire. He sits Dad down next to it, then comes back to help me.

"Good job, Maya," he says. I hand him my paddle. My hands are numb. I can't pull myself out of the boat. Saul leans over and puts his arms under mine. He lifts me out of my boat and carries me to shore. I let him.

I sink down next to Dad. Both of us reach our hands toward the fire. It's all we can do. Saul pulls at our clothes, takes off our wet sweaters and shoes. Dad and I sit like rag dolls.

My body is numb, but my mind whirls. "Who were those people, Dad?" I ask. "What were they doing? Why did he fight with you? Why did they take your boat?"

Saul hands Dad his dry hoodie, then takes my left hand and rubs it between his hands. My fingers flash with pain as blood rushes back into them.

Saul says, "The men are poachers. They've been cruising the coast all summer. They get into people's traps. They've been seen diving around here for sea urchins." He takes my other hand and rubs again. "They mean business, Maya. They probably planned to take Dad's boat. Josh Hampel had his motor tampered with. The Jacksons' nets were slashed. Our crab traps were emptied. That's how we found out about them." He pauses, then says, "And we've seen them swamp kayakers in their wake."

Dad nods. "Saul's right. You shouldn't be here."

"Why didn't you tell me?" I ask. My heart feels cold.

Saul and Dad look at each other. "Because we knew you'd try to help. We thought you'd worry about all the animals around here. We thought you'd try to get close to them and end up swamped. Or worse. We didn't want you to worry." Dad reaches out to put his hand on my shoulder. I lean away.

"Or to help," says Saul.

"You didn't trust me?" I ask. The tears that threaten to spill out of my eyes are angry.

Dad sighs. He turns away. "What are we going to do?" he says. He slumps over with his head in his hands. Saul looks out to the bay. The look on his face is bleak.

Things couldn't be worse. Dad and Saul have lost their boat. Dad found out that I came out in my kayak even after he told me not to. Sooner or later he's going to ask me what I was doing. There are poachers out there. And to top it off, Saul and Dad didn't trust me enough to tell me. The thought makes me choke. Only my exhaustion keeps me from screaming at them.

I stare out at the bay. I can't see the sea otters, but I know they're out there. The chill in my heart turns colder. The sea otters are in this bay because there's a bed of sea urchins here. If the poachers are diving for the sea urchins, they'll find the sea otters. Then things are going to get even worse.

A boat turns into the bay. Saul wades into the water and waves them toward us. "Mark, over here." It's the coast guard.

The three of us huddle in the wind as the boat speeds back to town. Mark unscrews a thermos and pours something hot into the lid. He hands it to Dad. "You went after the poachers, didn't you?" he says.

Dad nods.

"I told you to leave it to us. You shouldn't be out there."

Dad and I catch each other's eye. He leans over. Here it comes. He's going to ask me what I was doing. What am I going to say? Normally I'd tell him the truth.

Not today.

If they don't trust me, why should I trust them?

Instead of asking me anything, he puts his arm around me. "I guess we've both been caught, eh?"

I nod.

"But no more disobeying me, okay? We're agreed? You'll stay away?"

Dad is worried about the poachers. He's upset about losing his boat. He's cold and shocked and worn. Losing his boat is one of the worst things that can happen to him. The last thing he needs is to worry about me. So I nod again.

This time I'm not sure if I'm lying.

I can't stop thinking about Gertrude and Oscar and Lilly. If the poachers find them, what will they do? Will they shoot them? How am I going to keep the poachers away from the sea otters? I lean away from Dad's embrace. It might not be possible to stay away from Riley Bay.

"How come you haven't caught the poachers?" I ask Mark. My voice comes out harsh and angry. "If you were doing your job, none of this would be happening." I don't know if it's the coast guard I'm angry with, but I can't shout at Dad when he's so down.

"Maya," says Dad.

"It's okay, Gerry. I understand why she's upset. The thing is, Maya, we can't accuse someone of poaching unless we catch them doing something illegal or we find illegal catch on board."

"So catch them then," I say.

Saul laughs. "As if. It's not that easy, Maya. You saw what they're like."

I can see from their faces that this is what they all believe. I stand up and walk to the other side of the boat. There must be something we can do.

Chapter Eight

Mom freaks out. About everything.

"Poachers!" she says. "What are they looking for? Why would they steal the boat? What are we going to do?" She doesn't forget to ask, "What were you doing out there, young lady? You were supposed to be at school."

I'm about to confess. She's so upset, and Dad still looks like a zombie. I can't bear to lie to them anymore. I'm about to tell them everything when Saul walks in.

"Dad, what are we going to do without a boat?" he says. He slumps into the sofa and drops his head into his hands.

Dad closes his eyes and takes a deep breath, then says, "The coast guard will get the boat back in no time. We'll be fine."

None of us believes it. Not even Dad. He shakes his head and sinks down beside Saul. Mom and I don't move. Dad worked hard to afford that boat, and I don't want to think about what will happen if the coast guard can't find it.

Dinner is so quiet, we can hear the tide lap at the shore. Mom eats slowly, as if she's thinking. Dad slumps against the table and hardly eats at all. Saul stares at the candle in the center of the table. He shovels his food in without stopping. I eat, but I can't taste anything.

When we have finished with dinner, Mom clears the table and returns with four bowls and a tub of ice cream.

"We need this tonight, I think," she says.

Dad sighs. "I don't know what we're going to do. I put everything into that boat."

"Maybe I can get a job at the library," Mom says with a smile. We all know she won't make enough money to support the family and buy a new boat.

"You can't give up yet," Saul says to Dad. "There has to be something we can do." He flings his spoon into his bowl and sinks back into his chair.

Dad says, "I'll talk to the coast guard. I'll head over there right now. Maybe they'll find the boat." He leans over and puts his arm on Saul's shoulder. "It's a start, eh?"

Saul nods but doesn't look up until after Mom and Dad are gone. Saul and

I sit and listen to the car drive away. When we can't hear it anymore, Saul pushes his chair from the table and leaves the room.

I go to my room and lie on my bed. I stare at the ceiling. This morning I was worried about the sea otters, and that was all. I'm still concerned about them, even more now that I know there are poachers out there. But now I'm also anxious about my family.

How are we going to survive without a boat? What's Dad going to do? I'm sure that Dad's upset for Saul too. He was so excited that Saul was going to work with him this year. Now they're both out of work. Dad must feel terrible about that.

I roll over and bury my face in my pillow. I drift in and out of sleep. At some point, I dream I'm playing with sea otters and Dad's beside me in his own kayak. I wake up.

For a moment I'm happy. Then I remember what's happened. I wonder if I should tell Dad about the sea otters. It might make him feel better. But why should I make him feel better when he doesn't trust me?

He's lost everything. The truth hits me in the stomach. I lean over the bed and retch. The stench fills the room.

We've all lost everything.

When my stomach settles, I get a rag from the bathroom and clean up my mess. A million thoughts run through my head, so many I can't hold on to any of them.

Except one.

All night, the thought grows in my head. When I get out of bed in the morning, I have a plan.

It could backfire. I'm not sure if I should tell everyone about it. I walk down the stairs still undecided.

It's strange to eat breakfast with Saul and Dad. Usually they're long gone by now. Dad hasn't shaved. He sits in his housecoat and shovels in eggs. He doesn't look at me when I walk into the room. "Good morning," I say.

He looks up and grunts. Saul sits in his sweatpants and stares across the room.

"What did the coast guard say?" I ask Mom, since she actually smiles at me. She shakes her head. "Nothing useful."

"As usual," says Saul.

Dad gives Saul a stern look. "Enough. Mark works hard."

There's no other conversation at the table. The silence sits on our shoulders.

By the time I'm finished my eggs, I've made up my mind. I can't let my family go on like this, even if they don't trust me. It's unbearable.

"I have a plan," I say.

Everyone looks at me. I take a deep breath and start. "There are sea otters around here. They've been there for a week. I've gone out every morning to make sure they're okay." Mom and Saul both lean forward. "What if we let it out that there are sea otters around that are eating from a bed of sea urchins bigger than any other on the coast? The poachers will come looking, but we'll be there."

Dad and Saul exchange glances. Dad gets up and walks around the table. None of us speaks as he paces around us.

Finally he says, "It's an excellent idea, Maya. We'll hide under the tree branches and wait until they come. It's brilliant. We'll let the coast guard know and all the fishermen. We'll have a whole fleet of boats nearby in case they try to run for it."

My heart sinks. Dad thinks this is a good plan. That's great. But now

I know for sure I've put the sea otters at risk. The thought of Gertrude and Oscar and Lilly getting hurt makes my skin prickle.

"Wait," I say. "Before I tell you where the sea otters are, you have to promise to take care of them. I don't want anything happening to them."

Dad and Mom both nod. "Of course we will," says Dad.

"Don't you trust us?" asks Saul.

I look him in the eye. "Now you know how it feels," I say.

Mom says, "She's right, you know."

We all look at her in surprise.

"They didn't tell me either, Maya, so I know how you feel." She catches Dad's eye. He turns away. Then Mom asks, "Where are the sea otters, Maya?"

"They're in Riley Bay, where Saul was standing sentry."

Dad laughs. Saul says, "So that's why you were there." He shakes his head.

Dad rubs his hand along his chin. "Time to shave. I'll go to the coast guard office and tell them the plan. Then I'll go to the docks and talk about the sea otters."

"You should get to school, Maya. You can let people know about the sea otters there," says Mom. "I'll go grocery shopping and talk about the sea otters in town."

Saul looks at me with a frown on his face.

"What?" I ask, but he shrugs and walks away.

I stay at the table. It feels good to have a plan, but I'm still worried that I've done the wrong thing. What if something happens to Gertrude or Oscar or Lilly? I'll never forgive myself.

Chapter Nine

The next morning, two coast guard boats arrive at our dock before the sun rises. Dad and Saul step into one boat. I bend down to my kayak.

"No way, Maya," says Dad.

I pick up my life jacket and paddle, and I drag the kayak into the water.

"Maya," says Dad. "No way. You stay here. It's going to be dangerous out there."

"Like yesterday?" I ask.

"Like yesterday."

"Yesterday when I rescued you."

He opens his mouth and closes it again.

"She's right," says Saul.

"You keep out of this," says Dad. "Maya, you are a fourteen-year-old girl, and they are mean and dangerous men."

"He's right," says Saul, which is not at all helpful.

"I'll stay out of the way. I promise. I'll paddle along the shore like usual, and then I'll land and watch from there."

Dad shakes his head.

"I'll take my cell phone and my radio."

He shakes his head again.

Mom comes down to the dock with a thermos in her hand. Once she hears both of us, she says, "Have these men ever seen you, Maya?"

"No."

"Then they'll think you're just another kayaker. Let her go, Gerry."

Saul and I stare at her. Is this my mom speaking? She hands the thermos to Dad. "I thought about what you did yesterday, Maya. It was brave," she says.

Dad steps off the boat and pulls her away. They argue. I try not to listen.

I'm going, whether Dad wants me to or not. I have a promise to keep to Gertrude and Oscar and Lilly. But I want Dad to say I can come. I bite at my fingernails as I wait.

When Dad comes back, he says, "Stay out of the way. Promise?"

"Yes." That's a promise I can keep.

The coast guard boats roar off into the bay. I secure my cell phone in my pocket and my radio on the shoulder strap of my life jacket.

"Thanks, Mom," I say as I slip the boat into the water.

"Remember your promise," she says.

"I will."

The coast guard boats disappear around the headland, and I'm alone in the bay. It's like any other morning.

The sun hasn't risen above the horizon, but there is light. I can see the silhouettes of the hills around me. I paddle to the center of Riley Bay and search the water for the sea otters. It's hard to see in the dim light. I hear splashing to my left and head toward the sound. The sea otters ignore me as I paddle up to them. They play several feet away. I settle in to watch them. I place my paddle across my cockpit and lean into it. My radio crackles, and Dad's voice says, "You promised to stay out of the way, Maya."

I look around. The boats are well hidden under the trees. I can barely make out their shapes. With all the rocks and tiny islands in this bay, the poachers will never notice them.

The sea otters splash and twist in the water.

I long to stay with them.

But I did promise, so I paddle to shore and climb out of the boat. I hide it and find a tree to crouch behind.

As the sun rises, I stare through my binoculars. Like everyone else, I'm waiting for the poachers. When it's bright enough, I turn my binoculars to look at Dad and Saul in the coast guard boat. They seem nervous. Both of them are looking into the bay. They're both more still than usual. I watch them as much as I watch the bay.

When the sun's fully up, the coast guard boat slips out from under the trees and slowly motors to me.

Dad calls out, "They're not coming, Maya. Not now that the sun is up. It was a good plan. Too bad it didn't work." He shrugs. It's all over now.

"Go home now, please. Mom will be worried," is all he says.

The coast guard boats leave, and I'm alone in the cove. I paddle out to the sea otters, tears pouring down my cheeks. Everything has backfired. We didn't catch the poachers, and now everyone in town knows about the sea otters. What have I done?

The sun breaks over the treetops. Gertrude is eating a sea urchin. She cracks its shell and rolls over to clear the shell bits out of her fur, then nibbles on the flesh inside. Oscar and Lilly hang out nearby. My tears have dried. Watching the sea otters has that effect.

I'm about to head home before Dad or Mom regret letting me come out here when I hear an engine. It's not unusual, so I don't pay attention. Then the sound changes. I recognize the boat motoring into the bay.

It's the poachers.

Chapter Ten

Without thinking, I put my paddle in the water and sprint for shore. The poachers must have seen me. I was sitting right in the middle of the bay, far from any rock or island. My thoughts spin about. Are they following me? What will they do when they catch me? Should I radio for help? My mouth is dry and my breath is sharp. My arms push the paddle faster and the boat glides through the calm water. When I'm almost at shore, I risk a glance over my shoulder.

They've stopped in the bay.

They're not paying attention to me at all.

I let the kayak slow. I take a deep breath to clear my mind. Of course they haven't followed me. Why would they? As far as they know, I'm a kayaker out for a morning paddle. I drift closer to land. I'm shaking. I need to get to shore. Then an idea hits me.

I paddle around the headland, as if I was passing through. When I can't see the poachers' boat anymore, I pull my kayak up onto shore and walk to the other side of the headland, where I can see the poachers.

I search for a place to hide. I push aside a pine branch and crawl into the space behind it. It's like a nest. I'm surrounded by tree branches and small shrubs.

I brush away twigs and branches on the ground to smooth out a place to sit. I can see the poachers' boat clearly through the branches.

They have anchored in the middle of the bay.

Right where the sea otters hang out.

A sea otter watches them from the far side of the kelp bed. I bite my lip, then whisper a message, "Stay away from them. Stay away."

There are three men on board. One looks familiar. Even though it's a small bay, they're too far away for me to be sure of their faces. I fumble for my binoculars but remember they are in the kayak.

Two of the men are wearing dry suits and oxygen tanks. The other one stands near the motor. He keeps checking the water. The men in dry suits have long metal instruments that look like rakes in one hand and a mesh harvest bag in the other. They step to the edge of their boat and dive overboard.

I can hardly breathe. This is the worst thing that could happen. The poachers are hunting sea urchins. The sea otters are nearby, and they don't know how dangerous these men are.

If I got into my kayak and paddled out to the poachers, what would I do? I remember what happened to Dad. A wave of weakness travels down my legs at the thought. I'm not brave enough to go out there on my own.

I'm helpless, crouching here under the trees.

I can't see the sea otters clearly, but I can see when they roll over and their flippers splash. One moves closer to the divers.

Oh no!

I hold my breath until the sea otter swims away.

I can't believe I'm watching this, and there's nothing I can do.

Maybe there is something I can do. I have a cell phone with me. I can take pictures. They won't be great, but they will be something.

I shuffle closer to the water's edge. I'm still behind branches, but I can see more clearly. It's hard to get good photos with a cell phone, especially when the boat's moving on the water. I snap three of the man in the boat, but his back is turned.

"Turn, turn," I whisper.

One of the divers surfaces. I point my phone at him and wait. He raises a bag heavy with sea urchins. I wait until the right moment, then click. I take another picture, then another. Eventually the man in the boat turns, and I take a picture of his face.

After the diver hands over his bag, he dives back down. I wait for the next diver to surface. The sun is high now. It sparkles off the water. It's hard to see. That must be why I don't see the diver coming toward me until he is almost at the shore.

Something catches my eye close to shore. Bubbles. My brain can't make sense of it.

Bubbles?

Then I understand. The bubbles mean that someone is swimming underneath with an air tank. One of the poachers is heading to shore.

How does he know I'm here? Did he see the sun glint off my cell phone?

I put my hand over my mouth to stop myself from crying out. I back into the undergrowth. There's no time to run. He's almost at the shore.

The diver steps out of the water onto the sand right next to where I'm hidden. I hold my breath, but I'm sure he'll hear my heart thump or see me trembling. I hold on to a branch to steady myself.

The picture of Dad falling out of his boat is clear in my mind.

The poacher stands on the shore. He lays his rake and bag on the sand. He pulls off his air tank, tears off his hood and unzips his dry suit. He kicks off his flippers and turns toward me.

"Argggh," I say as I bite into my hand. His eyebrows crease, but he's still glancing about. He looks for me, but doesn't know where I am. I don't breathe. He shakes out his hair, and looks around again.

The man's eyes find what they are looking for. He thumps right toward me.

I have to take a breath. I move my hand and open my mouth to breathe in. I want to gulp air, but all I do is take a couple of quiet breaths, then clamp my hand over my mouth again.

He walks past.

Can he see me from behind? I don't dare look.

I hear nothing for a minute. The sound I hear next almost makes me laugh in relief. The man has come to shore to take a pee.

He hasn't seen me.

I breathe again but don't move my hand. He's still nearby.

When he finishes peeing, he walks back to his air tank. He zips up his suit and struggles into his air tank and flippers. He grabs his bag and rake and walks into the water.

The bubbles move away from shore. I flop to the ground. My hand shakes. I put my cell phone in my pocket so that no one will see the sun glint off it.

When I feel calm enough, I walk back to my kayak. I make it home in record time. All I want to do is get away from those men.

Chapter Eleven

By the time I get home, I can hardly crawl to the sofa. It feels soft on my exhausted body. I close my eyes and let my arms and legs flop. They weigh a ton.

Saul walks into the room carrying a plate of sandwiches and a glass of milk.

"What happened to you?" he asks.

I tell him.

He sits with a sandwich halfway to his mouth and listens. His face turns redder and redder as I talk. When I tell him about the poacher coming to shore, he drops his sandwich onto his plate.

"That's it," he says when I'm finished. "You're staying home from now on. What if he'd seen you?"

"Whatever," I say.

"I mean it. You're staying home."

"No way."

I am scared of the men. I know they're dangerous. But everything is at stake now. They know where the sea urchins are. They'll find the sea otters soon for sure. Dad's boat is gone. Saul and Dad have no work.

I know Saul is only trying to protect me, but I can take care of myself. I've proved that. I rescued Dad. I came up with the plan. I took photos of the men diving for urchins.

"You can't tell me what to do," I say.

He leaps out of his chair, sending sandwiches flying. He bends over me, points his finger in my face.

"Don't you get it? These men are dangerous. They pushed Dad off his boat. They've stolen things. They've swamped kayakers. You almost got hurt, Maya," Saul says, sitting back down.

"But I didn't."

"Not this time."

We glare at each other. Saul looks away first, but he says, "What good did it do?"

Then I smile. "I took photos."

"Of the poachers?"

I nod.

Saul shakes his head. "Okay, Maya, you win. But I'll be watching you."

"Deal. Actually, I never want to get close to those men again. Let's go upload those photos."

Saul gathers his sandwiches from the floor, and we go to the study.

There are three blurry photos of a person in a diving hood holding up a bag and three of a man on a boat on the screen. I enlarge the photos, but that makes them go pixely. "They're not good enough, are they?" I ask Saul.

He scrunches his sandwich into his mouth. "These could be taken anywhere, and those guys could be anyone. You can't see what's in the bags."

I take a slow breath. My limbs feel heavy again.

I know it's true.

"There's one more," I say. I click on the last photo. Saul and I gasp.

"I can't believe it," I say. I'm looking at the face of Mark, from the coast guard. I'm sure it's him. My ears burn, and I think I might throw up. Saul swears and punches his hand into the table.

"No wonder they didn't come today. No wonder the coast guard can't catch them. How could he?"

"I thought Mark and Dad were friends," I say.

"So did I. So did Dad."

"We've been betrayed." I lean back and put my hands over my eyes.

That's it. If Mark's one of the poachers, there's nothing we can do. I slam the laptop shut. But Saul opens it.

"Wait," he says. He sits, and I leave him staring at the computer.

We show Dad the photos when he comes home. His face drains to white. He shakes his head and sits heavily in the chair.

"I have a plan," says Saul. Before Dad can answer, he adds, "You go to Mark and tell him you've given up. Tell him you want the insurance money for the boat and that's all. He'll believe you. Meanwhile, Maya and I will go back to the cove with a proper camera and take photos."

"Not on your life," says Dad. He looks at us as if we've lost our minds. "Mom and I are going to drive to the city to talk to the police. I'm not letting Mark get away with it."

"What proof will you have?" asks Saul.

Dad points to the photo, but Saul says, "That just shows Mark in a boat. There's nothing wrong with that. You need proof."

"I don't want to talk about it anymore. Mom and I are going to the police."

When Dad's gone, Saul looks at me. "That's it, I guess."

But I know it isn't. Saul's right. It will be the Mark's word against Dad's, and Dad is just a fisherman. Why would the police believe him?

Chapter Twelve

Everything's gone wrong.

It's my fault the sea otters are in danger. I can't believe I've been this stupid. "Now the poachers know where the sea urchins are," I say. "It won't take long for them to notice the sea otters."

"Yeah," says Saul quietly.

"They'll capture them for sure."

I wait for Saul to say they won't, but he doesn't. He looks at me with a frown, then shakes his head. "I don't know. Maybe not." I can tell he doesn't believe himself.

"If Gertrude and Oscar and Lilly are captured, there will be no more sea otters around here," I say.

"I know."

We stand at the window. Neither of us moves.

"I can't bear it," I say.

Saul puts his hand on my shoulder.

"There has to be something we can do," I say.

"Like what?"

My body sags. "I don't know."

I lean my head against the window. "How long will the poachers be there?" I ask.

"Diving, you mean?"

"Yeah."

Saul thinks. "In this cold water with tanks, they'll be gone by now."

"Are you sure?" I ask.

He nods. "Positive."

"We should go and check on the sea otters," I say. I'm exhausted, and the last thing I feel like doing is getting into my kayak, but I have to do it. I just do.

He shakes his head. "You're crazy," he says.

My head spins. He's saying no.

"But you're right," he adds.

I sigh in relief.

"We can pull up on the headland and check to see if the poachers' boat is there first," I say.

"I'll go," says Saul suddenly.

I look at him and cross my arms. "You know I'm coming with you," I say.

He nods. "I had to try."

We pull Saul's kayak out from under the house, and the two of us head off in our boats. Mom and Dad have gone to the police, but I don't think that'll help. It's up to me and Saul.

When we reach Rugged Point, we beach our kayaks and hike over the headland to take a look. The bay is empty. Not a boat in sight.

We get back into our kayaks. We paddle into Riley Bay and around the rocks and islands.

"Gertrude, Oscar, Lilly," I call out.

"Gertrude," calls Saul. When I look at him funny, he shrugs and laughs. "I can't see them," he says.

"Keep looking. Maybe they're sleeping. Let's split up. I'll paddle on the north side of the bay, you look on the south side."

Saul nods and paddles away from me.

I turn my kayak and head toward the closest islet. I'm worried. What if the poachers found them already?

Cormorants drying their wings on the rock watch me circle around the islet. There are no sea otters here. I paddle across to the next rock and circle it. Still no sea otters.

"Gertrude," I call. Usually I find them easily, but not today. My throat tightens as I circle more rocks and islets and see no sign of sea otters.

When I reach the far end of the bay, I paddle under the overhanging tree branches just in case. No sea otters here.

What have I done?

I make my way along the shoreline, moving slowly. My eyes scan the logs and roots under the water. The sea otters must be here. They must.

They're not.

Saul's kayak comes out from behind a rock. I wave at him, "Saul, have you found them?"

He shakes his head and paddles away.

I follow the curve of the bay closely. Overhanging branches block my way.

Logs and driftwood have been shoved close to shore in the storms. It's hard to see, but up ahead there's a jumble of wood that looks weird. I can't tell what's different about it.

When I'm close enough to see properly, I shout, "Saul, SAUL! Help, I've found them." I glance over my shoulder, but it's no use. He's across the bay. The wind blows my voice away from him.

The three sea otters huddle in a group. I angle my boat toward them. As I glide closer, one of them, I can't tell if it's Lilly or Oscar, hisses at me.

I back away. Sea otters are wild creatures. They're dangerous.

I take another stroke toward them. Lilly hisses. I have to find out what's going on. Why are they all huddled up under the branches? It's a strange place for them.

I decide to try another approach. Instead of angling toward the sea otters,

I glide past them. Once I've drifted fifty feet, I change my angle and paddle slowly toward them. They're watching me, but they're not hissing or growling.

When I get twenty feet from the sea otters, I can see what the matter is.

Gertrude is wound up in a harvest bag. My whole body shakes when Gertrude turns her teddy-bear face and stares at me.

Now I know the worst has really happened.

The sea otters have been hurt by the poachers.

"Oh no," I groan. "Gertrude, what's happened to you?" I don't know what to do. Somehow I'm going to have to free Gertrude from the mesh of the bag, or she'll die. Her flippers are all caught up. She won't be able to swim or eat.

My mind whizzes in a million direc- tions. I'm panicking, like when I thought I'd lost Dad. I glance across the bay.

I wave and shout again, "Saul. SAUL…"
But he doesn't see or hear me.

I have to do something, and I have to do it now. Then I hear the sound I've been dreading. A motor. It's a boat coming in. In seconds, I see it round into the bay, heading right for me.

It's the poachers.

Chapter Thirteen

I have to get away from the sea otters so the poachers don't see them. I sprint for a rock to hide behind.

Why have they come back?

About sixty feet away from me, they cut their motor and stop. One of them leans over the side of the boat like he's looking for something. His bag, I bet. They must have noticed it was missing.

They'll be desperate to find it so no one knows they've been harvesting sea urchins out of season. I can't hear what they say, but I can see them arguing. Then two of them pull on dry suits and splash overboard.

My hand clutches my paddle. What if one of them swims over to the sea otters? He'll see Gertrude. Then what?

Without thinking, or even knowing I'm about to do it, I paddle out from behind the rock. I have no plan, but I have to keep them away from the sea otters.

"Hey," I call. My voice hardly comes out. I try again. "Hey." This time I'm louder. Mark looks at me.

"Hey, Maya, are you calling us?" he says.

I wet my lips and cough to clear my throat. "Are you looking for a harvest bag?"

He doesn't answer.

I cough again. "I saw a bag here earlier. Is it yours?"

Mark leans forward. The look in his eyes has changed. Before he was playing at being friendly. Now he knows that I know. He starts his engine. I've made a big mistake.

I was so concerned about the sea otters that I forgot to worry about myself. How could I be so stupid?

"Saul, over here!" I shout, but there's no answer.

There's a narrow channel between some rocks ten strokes behind me. If I can get in there, Mark won't be able to reach me. I paddle hard backward. The kayak wobbles and heads toward a rock. I correct my angle and try again. I'm still five strokes away from the channel.

Below me, I see a dark shape. At first I think it's a sea otter, but it is moving too slowly. Then I see bubbles, and I know exactly what it is. A diver.

I brace myself as the diver hauls himself up onto the stern of my boat. He flings his chest across my back hatch. His feet hang in the water. He leans sideways and tries to tip me.

I throw my weight the other way.

He leans his weight left. I fling mine right. Somehow I keep the boat upright. He growls at me. It doesn't sound like a human voice. He leans again. This time I go over.

The man lets go of my boat. He lunges at me underwater. I struggle to roll the kayak upright, but he's too close. He's got a rake in his hand.

He's coming right for my face.

A second before he hits me, something streaks by and knocks him out of the way. His tank falls to the sea floor below him. I'm running out of air, and I have no time to see what it was that hit him, so I set up my paddle and roll.

When I surface, Saul is sitting in his kayak beside me. He has his paddle in one hand and his radio in the other. He's checking underwater to see where the diver got to. Mark's boat is coming our way.

"Are you okay?" asks Saul. "I can't believe you just did that. What were you thinking?"

It's a good question, but we don't have time to think about it right now. The channel is right behind us, but we won't both fit. My head spins around, searching for a way out.

"Head behind a rock," I shout. Saul understands immediately. He grabs the bow of my boat and sweeps it around, changing my angle. He gives me a push. I take one stroke, and another and another. In five seconds Saul and I are surrounded by rocks.

"They're still coming," says Saul. It's true. Mark is motoring straight toward us.

I want to cry, but I need to keep my head.

I breathe deeply. My fingers grip my paddle so tightly my knuckles feel like they might crack. I've done the thing I most feared. I've put everything at risk. Me. Saul. The sea otters.

I look underwater. One of the divers still has a tank. He could be anywhere.

Then I see a shadow slide under the water. The bubbles rise to the surface. I thrash my paddle in his direction. He backs away.

When I look up, Mark is almost on me.

A wake rears off the back of Mark's boat. It sends a wave crashing over the rocks. Spray flies off into our faces. Our kayaks rock wildly. I grab at Saul's boat.

The wave passes, but Mark circles around again and another wave hits the rocks. The spray soaks us. Our boats rock, knocking into each other.

The diver swims up behind us, cutting off our escape from the rocks. Saul thrashes his paddle at him, but he only backs away a few feet.

"They're trying to corner us," I call to Saul. I'm so frightened I want to puke.

"Leave us alone," Saul shouts.

The boat doesn't even slow down.

Around it comes again. It's moving faster now. The wake is higher than our kayaks.

"Arghhhhhh…" I shout as the spray hits me.

"We have to get away from the rocks," Saul yells.

But we're too tight against the rocks to move. The swell from Mark's wake has pushed us so close to the rocks, we're in danger of being dashed against them. Our kayaks will break.

We'll be swamped.

Chapter Fourteen

A dark shadow swims at us from under the water again. I grasp my paddle, ready to thrash the diver. Then the dark shape flips, and Oscar's head appears. He swims into the path of Mark's boat.

He bares his teeth and growls.

Mark looks down and laughs. He bends down in the boat where we can't see him and reappears a second later with an oar in his hand.

"Get out of there, Oscar," I shout.

Mark turns to look at me, the oar still raised. In that moment I know he'll stop at nothing to get his net back.

He's coming for us, no matter what.

Oscar snarls and dives. He resurfaces a few feet farther away from Mark's boat. Mark swings at him again.

"Now," shouts Saul. He pushes my boat.

Together we sprint away from the rocks.

"Head for the kelp," says Saul.

"Oscar..." I shout.

"Can take care of himself. Now paddle," says Saul.

I have no choice. I paddle with every ounce of strength I have. My arms scream at me and my stomach muscles burn as we sprint across the bay.

Mark isn't distracted by Oscar for long. Before we reach the kelp, he zooms after us.

"Come on," shouts Saul. His boat pulls ahead of me. I paddle harder to keep up. The kayaks slide into the kelp bed and instantly slow.

"Keep moving," shouts Saul.

I have no intention of stopping.

I dig my paddle into the water and push. It slides through kelp strands. I twist the paddle as I pull it out of the water. Kelp streams off it.

We paddle deeper into the kelp bed. I dig my paddle into the water and pull it toward me. It catches on a strand of kelp. I flip it off my paddle. Another catches it. I can hardly move through the water, the seaweed is so thick.

"We can't paddle through this kelp," Saul yells.

"Keep going," I shout. He turns back to me and nods.

We paddle as hard as we can, deeper and deeper into the kelp bed. Dig, pull, unwrap the paddle. Dig, pull, unwrap.

We're hardly moving.

The boat is gaining on us by the second.

With a deep breath, I sink my paddle in the water again. It's heavy with seaweed. I'm moving as fast as I can, yet I feel like I'm crawling.

I can hear Saul panting. I don't dare turn my head to look at him. I just paddle and paddle and paddle. The sound of the motor gets closer.

"Move it," I gasp at Saul with the last of my breath.

Mark's boat is about to ram my stern when I hear the sound I've been listening for. The motor grinds and whines and then stops.

I pull my paddle and slide away from Mark's boat.

Mark guns the motor. Again it whines and stops. Wisps of smoke leak from the engine, and the smell of burning oil fills the air.

His propellers are tangled in the kelp.

The boat is dead in the water.

I lift my paddle out of the water and take a deep breath. "That was close," I say.

"It's not over yet," Saul pants. He points, and I look around in time to see the diver's head sink below the surface at the edge of the kelp bed.

I grip my paddle and scan the water.

"I can't see him," I shout.

We search for a sign to show us where he's gone. Then I see movement in the kelp bed. It could be Oscar or Lilly, or it could be the diver.

Saul's seen it too. "Move it," he shouts at me. "Paddle away from me, as fast as you can. Splash a lot. He won't know which of us to follow," he says.

I dig my paddle into the water, and the kayak inches forward through the kelp. The diver must be gaining on me. I dig my paddle in again. Sweat pours into my eyes. I glance behind me. Saul has reached the edge of the kelp bed and is speeding away from me. There are bubbles behind him.

"Saul, behind you," I shout.

He turns and looks at the water, then plants his paddle and spins his boat around.

I struggle to turn my boat around in the kelp, but I'm too slow. The diver is only a few feet away from Saul.

Saul leans over as far as he can and swings his paddle through the water. A dark shape slices past.

"He's trying to get under you," I say.

Saul swipes his paddle through the water again.

"I hit him," Saul shouts.

The diver backs away. He surfaces, then turns and heads for me. I'm still in the kelp.

"Head to shore," shouts Saul, but I'm already moving, and I paddle harder than I ever have until I reach the edge of the kelp bed. Once I'm in clear water, my kayak surges forward, and in seconds I slip under the overhanging branches close to shore. The diver's bubbles are close behind me. I could grasp them in my hand. Twigs and needles slash across my face as I race along the shore.

"Go, Maya," shouts Saul from behind me, so I take another stroke and another and another. Then at last Saul says, "Maya, you can stop."

I glance back. The diver rises to the surface. He tears off his mask.

We stare at each other. My breath comes in ragged hunks. My fingers ache, and there's no strength left in my arms. I want to fling my paddle away and collapse over the deck of my kayak.

But there's something about the way he's looking at us.

"What's he doing?" Saul calls.

The man puts his mask back on and submerges. His bubbles drift away from us.

I wait for relief to flood my body. It doesn't. The bubbles head away from the boat. Toward the sea otters.

"He's heading to Gertrude!"

Chapter Fifteen

"We have to get there first." Saul pulls up beside me. He shoves my kayak. "Come on."

I dredge up some strength and follow him. The bubbles are ahead of us.

Strength comes from nowhere. Our kayaks fly across the water.

We reach Gertrude first.

Gertrude is lying in a huddle. Her head bumps shore each time a wave comes in. The sight of her wrapped up in the mesh of the bag makes my stomach lurch.

The water's murky here, and it's hard to see underwater. I keep my eyes open for bubbles, but they're hard to keep track of with the surge of the waves. There's a lot of driftwood and roots here.

That gives me an idea.

"Saul, send him toward me."

"What?"

"Just do it!"

Saul leans over and swishes his paddle through the water. The bubbles stop.

They start up again. Saul paddles up behind him and drags his paddle through the water again. The bubbles stop, then move back toward me. Saul follows. He blocks the diver from behind.

I paddle forward, making as much noise as I can.

The bubbles move away from me, closer to shore. My paddle catches in roots and driftwood. It slows me down. I pull my paddle loose and start again.

We herd the diver closer and closer to shore.

"Head for that tree," I tell Saul.

He changes the angle of his boat. We glide forward.

There are roots and logs all around us. The diver's moving more slowly now. He's trying to find his way through them.

"Keep going," I call out.

Saul nods.

We push the diver closer to the tree. Its branches scrape at our faces.

Finally, the bubbles stop moving.

"He's caught in the roots. He can't move," says Saul.

The diver stands up. He takes off his mask and glares at us.

"Don't think this is over," he says.

We don't answer.

He tugs at his tank. It's caught on the roots. "What are you going to do? Sit there forever?" he snarls.

"We don't have to," says Saul. "Just until the police get here."

"The police?" I ask.

"Of course."

"You radioed them?" I ask.

"Yeah. As soon as I saw the poachers' boat turn into the bay. They should be here any second."

The flood of relief washes over me from my toes all the way to my fingertips.

Chapter Sixteen

Dad and the police arrive a few minutes later. Mark and one diver are in the boat. The other diver stands in the water. He's got nowhere to go.

Saul and I tell the whole story. The policewoman calls for a fisheries officer to come and rescue Gertrude.

"We'll keep that bag as evidence," she says.

"They probably still have urchins on board," says Dad. The policewoman nods and speaks into her radio.

Saul and I ride home in the police boat. I don't have enough strength left to paddle a kayak.

"It's hard to believe this all happened in one day," I say. "Poor Gertrude. I wonder what's going to happen to the sea otters. I really screwed up."

I must look thoughtful, because Dad says, "Maya, telling us about the sea otters is the best thing you could do."

"It is?"

"Sure," he says, and he reaches over to take my hand. "Honey, now that everyone knows the sea otters are here, no one can hurt them, can they?"

He's right. When no one but me knew they were there, anyone could have hurt them and no one would hear about it. Now everyone will know if something happens to them. They're protected by that. I smile. "You're right, Dad. I should have thought of that."

He leans over and looks me in the eye. "You should have trusted all of us, eh?"

I nod. But then I say something that's been on my mind since all of this began. "You should have trusted me too, Dad. You should have told me about the poachers. I wouldn't have gone out there at all if I'd known there were poachers about. You should have told me."

Dad looks down at his shoes. When he looks back at me, he nods.

In the morning Dad and Saul and I paddle into the bay as the sun tips over the tree-tops. We spread out and check the whole bay. The sea otters are gone. I knew they would be, but I was hoping anyway.

I meet Dad back in the middle of the bay. My face must look pretty glum because Dad says, "Gertrude will be okay, you know."

I laugh. "You know I call her Gertrude?"

"Saul told me."

I blush, but then I think of Saul calling out to Gertrude. "Saul was awesome yesterday," I say.

"You should tell him that," says Dad.

I nod. "I will."

Saul paddles out from behind a rock and glides up beside us. "Sorry, Maya, no sight of them."

"It's okay. I know the fisheries guys will keep an eye on them," I say.

"Dad and I can watch for them when we're fishing," says Saul.

"Really? Fishing? You got your boat back?" I ask.

Dad shakes his head. "Not yet, but if the police don't find it, the insurance will cover the cost of replacing it.

In the meantime, Saul and I can crew on Johansen's boat."

"You can let me know where the sea otters are and how Gertrude is doing," I say. "If they're close enough, I'll paddle out before school and say hello."

"Sounds like a plan," says Dad. "For now, though, we'd better head back."

Saul and Dad and I put our paddles in the water. The sun is bright over our shoulders. The water sparkles as the three of us head home.

Kari Jones is a college instructor who teaches students to write, but when school is out, she can often be found with her family and friends exploring the natural world and dreaming up adventures to share. Kari lives in Victoria, British Columbia.

orca *currents*

The following is an excerpt from
another exciting Orca Currents novel,
Storm Tide by Kari Jones.

978-1-55469-807-3 $9.95 pb

Alone for the first time on
the island he calls home, Simon is looking forward
to a day of swimming and slacking off. His sister
Ellen only wants to make sure they get their chores
done. Neither Simon nor Ellen is prepared for the
mysterious and potentially dangerous visitor who
brings with him an unexpected storm and a riddle
that may lead to treasure. Simon and Ellen have
to work together to solve the riddle before the
stranger—or the weather—destroys their chances.

Chapter One

Today is going to be great. I head down to the dock to wave goodbye to Mom and Dad. They're going to Victoria for the day. That means that apart from my sister Ellen, who doesn't really count, I am totally alone on the island for the whole day.

On my way back to the house, I plan my day. I can do whatever in the world

I want. I've lived on this island all twelve years of my life, and this is the first time I have been alone on it for an entire day. If it warms up, I'm going to swim in the water hole. Then I want to check out the spring salmon run off Rudlin Bay.

First I need a couple of sandwiches, one for right now and one to take with me. I'm going to start the day with a hike to the midden on the other side of the island. A midden is basically an ancient First Nations garbage dump. That sounds gross, but it's actually really cool. All the gross stuff has decomposed by now, and all that's left are shells and bones covering a long stretch of beach. I go over there sometimes and sift through it. I have a good collection of bones from that site. But first things first, it's time to head inside for a snack.

Unfortunately, as I pull the ham and cheese out of the fridge, Ellen walks in.

"What are you doing?" she asks.

Ellen's voice has this mocking edge that would normally tick me off, but the last thing I want today is to fight with her, so I answer simply, "Making a sandwich."

"I can see that, Simon, but why?" Ellen says. This time there's no ignoring the you-are-so-stupid tone in her voice.

"I'm hungry." *Duh!* I don't say that out loud. I don't want to risk my day of freedom, after all.

"*That* hungry?" she points to the huge amount of food.

You'd think she could figure it out, but I patiently explain that I'm making food to last a while.

"What about your chores?" she says.

"What about them?" I ask.

Ellen puts her hands on her hips and stands between me and the fridge. I'm uncomfortable with where this conversation is going. I don't want to fight with Ellen today, but I can see my plans for the day disappearing if I let her tell me what to do.

"Mom and Dad expect the chores to be done. We're the keepers while they're away. They've got enough to worry about. You are not going anywhere until you've done your chores."

I hate it when Ellen speaks to me like that. But I have to admit it's true. Mom and Dad have a hard day ahead of them. The government's been closing lighthouses all around here. Dad is sure Discovery Island Lighthouse Station is next. He and Mom are going to tell the people at the ministry about all the things they do: rescue boaters, keep weather records and help the biologists collect data on waves and currents. Man, I hope they can convince them that the lighthouse station should stay open. This is my *home*!

"I'll have lots of time for chores," I say. I start spreading mustard on the bread.

Ellen stands there and watches me. She looks so much like Mom right now. Mom doesn't have to say anything. She has this look. Ellen has it too. Someday my sister is going to make one scary mother. I look back at her, trying to ignore the Mom look, but it's useless. The look is working. I can feel it.

"Okay, okay, I'll do my chores first," I say.

"You'd better. Then you can do whatever you want." Ellen smiles sweetly.

Ha.

My main job is the boat shed. I keep it tidy so we can pull the boats in quickly during storms. I was rummaging in the shed looking for my fishing rod yesterday, so I know exactly how messy it is. This is going to take forever, half an hour at least!

I start with the ropes. I coil them properly and hang them in their spot on the wall. Then I organize the crab traps and the motor parts and oars and paddles and life jackets. After a while I start thinking that something feels different. I can't put my finger on what it is, but something is out of place. I feel like I've half noticed something, but it's taking a while to get into my brain. I look around. Everything looks the same, doesn't it? What's different?

I walk back to the entrance of the shed and look outside. Nope. Everything looks right there—the rubber tire that we use as a bumper on the dock, the bucket and hose we keep for rinsing salt water off our gear. There's a barrel of strawberries Mom planted to make the place prettier. I turn back to the shed and look around inside. Everything is in the shed that should be. Isn't it? Maybe it's just my imagination.

I put this thought out of my mind and finish cleaning. When I'm done, I step onto the wooden planks leading from the shed to the dock. And I figure out what is missing.

A chill creeps up my back. I swear, when I walked into this shed half an hour ago, there were muddy footprints on the dock. They aren't there now.

orca currents

For more information on all the books
in the Orca Currents series, please visit
www.orcabook.com